The Authentic Life of Billy the Kid

A Play in Two Acts

Lee Blessing

A Samuel French Acting Edition

SAMUELFRENCH.COM
SAMUELFRENCH-LONDON.CO.UK

Copyright © 1979 by Lee Blessing
All Rights Reserved

The Authentic Life of Billy the Kid is fully protected under the copyright laws of the United States of America, the British Commonwealth, including Canada, and all other countries of the Copyright Union. All rights, including professional and amateur stage productions, recitation, lecturing, public reading, motion picture, radio broadcasting, television and the rights of translation into foreign languages are strictly reserved.

ISBN 978-0-573-64027-8

www.SamuelFrench.com
www.SamuelFrench-London.co.uk

For Production Enquiries

United States and Canada
Info@SamuelFrench.com
1-866-598-8449

United Kingdom and Europe
Theatre@SamuelFrench-London.co.uk
020-7255-4302

Each title is subject to availability from Samuel French, depending upon country of performance. Please be aware that *The Authentic Life of Billy the Kid* may not be licensed by Samuel French in your territory. Professional and amateur producers should contact the nearest Samuel French office or licensing partner to verify availability.

CAUTION: Professional and amateur producers are hereby warned that *THE AUTHENTIC LIFE OF BILLY THE KID* is subject to a licensing fee. Publication of this play(s) does not imply availability for performance. Both amateurs and professionals considering a production are strongly advised to apply to Samuel French before starting rehearsals, advertising, or booking a theatre. A licensing fee must be paid whether the title(s) is presented for charity or gain and whether or not admission is charged. Professional/Stock licensing fees are quoted upon application to Samuel French.

No one shall make any changes in this title(s) for the purpose of production. No part of this book may be reproduced, stored in a retrieval system, or transmitted in any form, by any means, now known or yet to be invented, including mechanical, electronic, photocopying, recording, videotaping, or otherwise, without the prior written permission of the publisher. No one shall upload this title(s), or part of this title(s), to any social media websites.

For all enquiries regarding motion picture, television, and other media rights, please contact Samuel French.

Please refer to page 51 for further copyright information.

CAST

PAT F. GARRETT—57, rancher, ex-sheriff, the man who killed Billy the Kid.

ASHMON UPSON—in his 70's, frontier journalist, ghost writer of Garrett's book, *The Authentic Life Of Billy The Kid*.

BILLY—in his 40's, a driver.

JIM P. MILLER—in his late 20's, rancher, Methodist deacon, hired killer.

PLACE

Pat Garrett's ranchhouse, 20 miles east of Las Cruces, New Mexico, in the Organ Mountains.

TIME

The evening of February 28, 1908—the night before Garrett was ambushed and killed on his way down to Las Cruces.

The Authentic Life Of Billy The Kid

ACT ONE

The interior of PAT GARRETT's *ranch house. There is a table Center, a sideboard Left. Near the sideboard, a shotgun hangs on the wall. Windows Right and Upstage. A fireplace in the Downstage Right corner. Three chairs at the table, stump by the fire. A door to the outside Up Right. It's a room in which a man has lived alone for some time. Comfortable for him, if not for more.*

PAT *sits on the stump, staring into the fire. He finishes some coffee, rises, goes to get his handgun, which hangs in a holster below the shotgun. He sits at the table, begins polishing the gun with a cloth.*

A knock at the door. A pause. Another knock. PAT *stares at the door. Slowly, a man opens the door, pokes his head in. It is* ASH UPSON.

ASH. Pat? (ASH *is halfway in the door. He stands shivering. Beneath his overcoat, he wears an ill-fitting and worn suit coat with an old plaid vest. A tattered derby, baggy trousers. White hair, sidewhiskers.*) Pat? You in here? (*Suddenly* PAT *stands, aims the gun at him.* ASH *recoils.*)

PAT. Why don't you just come right on in? (*Slowly* ASH *comes in, shuts the door.*) Who the hell are you?

ASH. (*Surprised.*) You know me.

PAT. No.

ASH. I'm Ash.

PAT. Ash?

ASH. Ash Upson. Pat, it's me. Bet you never thought you'd see me again.

PAT. You don't . . .

ASH. (*Smiling, advancing a step, starting to unbutton his coat.*) Pat? (PAT *cocks the gun.* ASH *freezes.*)

PAT. . . . look like him.

ASH. (*With a nervous laugh.*) Well, maybe not, but I sure as hell *am* him. You really don't recognize me? (*Pause.*) Guess I must've changed. (*Pause.*) You're a little different, too. Fifteen years. (*Pause.*) Pat, *look* at me. (PAT *studies his face.*) Now, what do you see?

PAT. (*Starting to recognize him.*) Ash?

ASH. That's right.

PAT. Ash Upson?

ASH. (*Smiling.*) I'm alive. Hair's all white, but it's me.

PAT. (*Dropping the gun to his side.*) My God, Ash Upson.

ASH. That's right.

PAT. I'll be damned.

ASH. Can I sit down?

PAT. (*A broad smile.*) Ash Upson! I never thought I'd see you again.

ASH. Well, you goin' to make me stand all night?

PAT. Well, no—sit down. You must be cold.

ASH. (*Sitting by the fire.*) Well I am, I admit.

PAT. (*Putting his gun back in its holster.*) Are you hungry?

ASH. No thanks. Nothing right now. Anyway, I guess I've had enough meals off you to last forever.

PAT. I guess you have. Still, you're welcome . . .

ASH. No, no. I'm fine for now. (*A pause. They stare at each other.*)

PAT. Can't believe it's you. (*They laugh together, awkwardly.*)

ASH. Oh, it's me all right. Can't believe you could forget me. I stayed with you so long.

PAT. Years.

ACT I   AUTHENTIC LIFE OF BILLY THE KID   7

ASH. (*Uncomfortably.*) It was years, wasn't it? I guess I owe you some back rent. (*They laugh as before.*)

PAT. I could use it.

ASH. Is that so?

PAT. Uh . . . well, I can always use another dollar.

ASH. So can I. So this is where you're living now.

PAT. I know it's small . . .

ASH. I've seen grander. Heard you owe money on it.

PAT. (*Surprised.*) Well, that's true.

ASH. I talked to some people down in Las Cruces. And they said a few things.

PAT. Well, you can't always believe folks down there . . .

ASH. Oh, I get my facts straight, Pat. Old reporter's habit. I've been following you right along. Like that time you just had to introduce your old friend Tom Powers to President Roosevelt, and told him Tom was a wealthy cattle owner. Tom Powers! The only thing he owned was a saloon. (*Laughs.*) You introduced Teddy Roosevelt to the proprietor of the Coney Island Popular Resort of El Paso, Texas. (*Pauses.*) So, I guess I have kept up on you, in a way. You want to know why I came up?

PAT. Well, naturally, I . . .

ASH. Something's happened. An important . . . event. And I'm here to tell you about it.

PAT. What kind of an . . .

ASH. I just want to put it squarely to you and leave.

PAT. Put what?

ASH. An offer. A project. And I simply want you to hear it and decide, that's all.

PAT. What is it? Some kind of offer for the ranch?

ASH. No.

PAT. (*Jokingly, but potentially serious.*) Because it's a hell of a ranch. At least, it could be. Of course, you'd have to get in line. I've got a man from Texas interested in it. A Mr. Miller. Tomorrow, we're going to . . .

ASH. Pat, I've seen the ranch. No, what I have in mind . . . you got a match? (PAT *supplies one, and* ASH *lights a cigar. He offers* PAT *one.* PAT *declines.*) Now, I think if we're going to talk projects, if we're going to talk offers, we've got to be honest with each other. You're in money trouble.

PAT. (*Pausing.*) Not really. A little.

ASH. A lot. That's what I heard. Let's face it, you've been sliding downhill financially for some time.

PAT. That's not true.

ASH. It sure as hell is! It's what you always do. Say, have you got something for a man to drink?

PAT. (*Going to the sideboard.*) Oh! Sure. Don't know why I didn't offer . . . (PAT *opens a drawer and produces a bottle of whiskey. He takes it and two glasses back to the table, pours drinks.*)

ASH. This is something, isn't it, Pat? Pair of old friends getting together again?

PAT. Old friends.

ASH. Long ago. We were poor, but we were never happy, eh? (ASH *laughs.* PAT *laughs.*)

PAT. Things were all right.

ASH. No, they weren't. You know why? We never understood the West. It's mostly gone now, of course. But at the time, we never understood the West is what you make of it. That's all it is. Outside of that it doesn't exist. We failed to become men of means. A man's got to have means, or he . . . or he falls apart.

PAT. Well, money helps.

ASH. Sure it does. Why Pat, if you had money, you wouldn't have to live like this.

PAT. This is temporary . . .

ASH. It could be permanent. (PAT *stares at his drink.*) Easy for a man to fool himself. Especially when he's young, dumb and poor like we were. Eventually he's just old and poor.

ACT I AUTHENTIC LIFE OF BILLY THE KID

PAT. (*Refilling the glasses.*) Here's to you.

ASH. (*He downs his drink in one gulp.*) Thanks. Damn good.

PAT. (*Laughing.*) My God, you *are* alive.

ASH. (*Squarely, seriously.*) Are you poor?

PAT. (*After a moment.*) Yes, I am.

ASH. Well, then, let's do something about it!

PAT. Well, if you can . . .

ASH. (*Standing.*) And the first thing I'm going to do is bring in that poor son of a bitch driver of mine. Told him I'd wave him in if you were being hospitable. That all right?

PAT. Sure. You got a driver with you?

ASH. 'Course. You don't think an old man like me'd drive all the way up here in the mountains alone, do you?

(ASH *smiles, opens the door and disappears. He returns with* BILLY, *who is cold, shivering. He is dressed in clothes of an ordinary cowhand. A serape, and a plain, broadbrimmed—but not ridiculously so— sombrero.* PAT *watches as* ASH *brings* BILLY *in and sits him in front of the fire.* ASH *starts for the whiskey bottle, then thinks better of it, and instead gives* BILLY *a small bottle from his coat.*)

ASH. There, try and warm up with that first. It'll get you to where you can appreciate the real stuff.

PAT. What's that?

ASH. Hostetter's Bitters. (BILLY *swigs, almost puts out the fire spitting the stuff out again.*) I've grown to hate the stuff myself, but it comes in a convenient-sized bottle. (*Of* BILLY.) He'll be all right. Just let him get warmed up.

PAT. What's his name?

ASH. Him? Barlow. Now, let's get back to business. We've got some things to discuss . . .

(BILLY *suddenly rises, goes to the whiskey bottle, pours himself a drink, sits again.*)

PAT. You get him in town? Or does he always drive for you?

ASH. Him? Always. Now look, Pat . . .

PAT. You travel a lot now?

ASH. Some.

PAT. Well, what do you . . . *do* now, Ash? Exactly. You doin' well?

ASH. Pretty well.

PAT. You can pay a driver. He dependable?

ASH. Pat, what is it you want to know?

PAT. I don't know. You know so much about me. What about you? What do you *do?* You still working for newspapers?

ASH. No. I . . . well, what do you care?

PAT. Friendly interest.

ASH. (*Rising in response to an impatient gesture from* BILLY, *circling.*) All right, then. No longer am I a simple boomer, travelling from frontier newspaper to frontier newspaper. No more writing down the tedium of daily life in Lincoln, Cimarron, Roswell, Mesilla and Las Cruces, just waiting for one man to walk into a saloon, order a drink and have his head blown off—that's happened, Pat. I've seen it. (*Pauses, regards* BILLY.) Well, no more of that. I am out of that now. Now, Patrick Floyd Garrett, now I am a full-time novelist.

PAT. Oh, shit!

ASH. No, it's true. I now write novels, under a variety of names, about the true West: its heroes, its devils, the men I know and knew and those I never met.

PAT. Novels?

ASH. Well, slightly fictionalized accounts of the great men of the American West . . .

PAT. Dime novels.

ASH. Hardly. My writings . . .

PAT. Goddamn yellow-back dime novels without a line of truth in them. (*A pause. They stare at each other.*)

ACT I AUTHENTIC LIFE OF BILLY THE KID 11

Ash. Well, occasionally, when I've got a deadline to meet . . .

Pat. The same shit you turned out about the Kid in our book, that you made me sign my name to!

Ash. You should be proud to have your name on that book! Besides, my name wouldn't have sold two copies.

Pat. It didn't sell two copies, anyway.

Ash. Pat, there was a lot of truth in your book. All through it, in fact.

Pat. *My* book! Hell, you wrote every word!

Ash. But it was your story, Pat. You told me the facts, and I put them into proper form.

Pat. Proper form! You mean all bent out of shape! There must be ten lies to the page. (*To* Billy.) He's a hell of a good liar.

Ash. Not lies. Heightenings. There's a difference.

Pat. Heightenings! Where is that thing? (Pat *starts towards the sideboard, stops, goes towards the fire and picks up his copy of the book from where it rests on the floor near the stump.*)

Ash. (*Pleasantly surprised.*) You been reading it lately?

Pat. Just like to take it out now and then to count the lies. (*Slapping the book.*) You can't prove to me a word is true before the part where I come in on the case.

Ash. (*Taking the book from* Pat, *reading the title page.*) "The Authentic Life Of Billy, The Kid, the noted desperado of the Southwest, whose deeds of daring and blood made his name a terror in New Mexico, Arizona, and Northern Mexico. A Faithful and Interesting Narrative. By Pat F. Garrett, Sheriff of Lincoln County, New Mexico, by who he was finally hunted down and captured by killing him."

Pat. You've got a whole novel right there. Too bad you didn't leave it at that.

Ash. I don't see why you're complaining. Compared to the rest of the books coming out then, this was indeed a faithful account. Why, some of those books had the Kid riding all over the West, killing a hundred men, and made him look like some kind of pasha whenever he went to Fort Sumner—with every woman in town hovering around him, holding the family jewels with one hand and lifting up her skirts with the other. (BILLY *has drained his glass, sighs pleasantly, smacks his lips.*)

PAT. Well, at least you never exaggerated a thing.

ASH. I didn't say that . . .

PAT. You better not. (*To* BILLY.) You ever read our book? (*Taking the book.*) Listen: "Let us return to the Kid, whom we left in imminent peril. He had only his trusty six-shooter and a short dirk . . . (ASH *winces.*) to make a fight against twenty well-armed savages." Didn't give much of a damn about odds, did he? "As the Kid darted up the apparently inaccessible cliff, the Indians quickly disappeared behind a friendly ledge, while a yell of baffled rage went up as only an Apache can utter, and lead rained against the mountainside."

ASH. You finished?

PAT. Hell, no. You ain't. "One brave, who appeared to possess the climbing abilities of the panther, quickly reached a point but a few feet beneath . . ." (BILLY, *very interested, has been leaning forward on the stump, and he now loses his balance and falls to the floor. He gets up hurriedly, sits.*) Hell of a story, Ash. Has 'em dropping like flies. (*Reading.*) "For one instant an arm and hand projected from the concealing ledge, a flash, a report, and the bold climber . . . a death-cry on his lips, reeled and fell backward, bounding from ledge to ledge, until he lay, a crushed and lifeless mass, at the feet of his band." It's exciting, Ash. You do paint a picture. I'd go on, but you start quoting that goddamn poetry again. (*Examining* ASH, *who sits quietly.*) Say Ash, how'd you find out about all this with the Apaches? I always meant to ask you. Where were you when it happened? Sounds like you were right up on that cliff, loading the Kid's gun for him.

ASH. Well, I . . . . I wasn't quite that close to things. I never heard about it until, oh, a year or two later.

PAT. Who told you?

ASH. The kid, naturally.

PAT. Where'd he tell you?

ASH. In a saloon.

PAT. Thank you. That sure clears it up. I never thought you invented all those lies yourself.

ASH. They were not lies! They were truer than truth! You never understood that, did you, Pat? Every word I wrote came out of the Kid's mouth. Besides, it all made you look better. Pat, Billy was a phenomenal man. You and I were lucky to know him. Without him, you'd have been just another sheriff, and I wouldn't have been allowed to chronicle the deeds of one of the great killers of the American Southwest. As I look back on it, I begin to regret you shooting him. He was the single greatest money-making enterprise in New Mexico.

PAT. What are you talking about?

ASH. I don't know for sure. Just if we'd been able to keep the Kid alive and take him East, put him on exhibit . . . Oh, I suppose I don't really mean to bring it up, now that you're in such a hole . . .

PAT. I am not in a *hole*.

ASH. Financially.

PAT. I haven't made the money I wanted to make. I've tried. I'm making it. I'll make it.

ASH. Not sitting here, you won't! I ought to know.

PAT. I've spent 25 years expecting the next deal to make me the man I . . . expect to be.

ASH. I know that. I know that. Pat, you're a good man, you're deserving. But I'm damn old, and I've seen a lot of men fail. Most men only fail once. With you, it's practically a form of religion. Here, have a cigar. (ASH *gives him one, lights it.*) Your biggest mistake ever was killing the Kid.

PAT. What?

ASH. You should never have killed him. It was a bad mistake.

PAT. What are you talking about? That made me famous. That made *me*.

ASH. Sure, Pat . . .

PAT. It *made* me. You shut up a minute, because there are a few things I know about. Everybody in New Mexico has heard my name. Everybody in the country, and it's because I killed Billy. There must be six damn books a year coming out about me and the Kid. I've been a presidential appointee. It's an accident that I never made money. That's all it is. And it's no mistake that I killed Billy. (*Pauses.*) Sometimes I think it through, how I shot him. I think if I should have . . . given him a warning. Well, I shouldn't have. And I wouldn't if I had to do it again. And I would kill him 50 times if I had to. I am a famous man.

ASH. I know, I know. You're famous. But just let me ask you one question: Fame is what you've got. Now, what do you *want*?

PAT. I know what I want.

ASH. What is it?

PAT. What do you care?

ASH. It's business.

PAT. (*Pauses.*) I want to . . . get out all right. I mean, I've lived a good life—a famous life, at least—and I want to finish it on . . . the same note.

(BILLY, *unwatched by the others, has walked around the room, and at one point quietly removed* PAT's *pistol from its holster. He now points it, apparently to test the aim, just above their heads. Suddenly the gun fires, breaking a bowl on the opposite side of the room.* PAT *rises instantly, grabs the shotgun and aims it at* BILLY. ASH *rises also, rushes between them.*)

ASH. (*To* BILLY.) What's wrong with you!? He'll be all

right, Pat. Just looking at your gun there, that's all, and it went off. Right? (BILLY *nods. To* PAT.) See?

PAT. Get him out of here!

ASH. (*He takes the gun from* BILLY.) No . . . Pat . . . He's sorry. Aren't you? (BILLY *nods. To* PAT.) Honest. Just a little mistake, that's all. Sit down. (BILLY *does so.* PAT *puts the shotgun back.*) Just an accident. Sit down, Pat. Please. He'll be all right. He'll be fine. (ASH *gives* PAT *the pistol.* PAT *sits.* ASH *laughs nervously.*) Here I've been here this long and I haven't even put it to you yet.

PAT. What?

ASH. My project! Listen to me. You and I both know the best thing you ever were—the only thing you were ever good at—was sheriffing.

PAT. I was passable.

ASH. You were a born sheriff! The world knows you as a sheriff. And what does the world know about you as a sheriff? That you killed Billy.

PAT. Ash, you're going in circles.

ASH. Well, now I'm going to pounce. Drink up. I got a little surprise for you. (ASH *walks to* BILLY.) How you doing? Still cold? (BILLY *shivers.*) You'll get over it. (*To* PAT.) He's been colder than this. He still remembers the time he was holed up in that little frozen stone house at Stinking Springs for the longest, coldest day of his young life. (*To* BILLY.) Don't you?

PAT. Stinking Springs? When was he there?

ASH. Same time you were, Pat.

PAT. (*Looking at* BILLY.) We cornered five men at Stinking Springs. None of 'em named Barlow.

ASH. Well, I lied a little about the name. Truth is, he *was* one of those five poor hungry boys. Guess which one.

PAT. I killed one of them right there—Charlie Bowdre.

ASH. (*Laughing.*) Well, it's not Charlie Bowdre. We're not resurrecting any ghosts here.

PAT. And it's not Dave Rudabaugh. He's in Mexico. You must know that.

ASH. No, it isn't Dave Rudabaugh, either.

PAT. (*Rising, growing irritated with the game.*) Billy Wilson?

ASH. No, but you're sneaking up on it.

PAT. This is stupid.

ASH. Just guess.

PAT. Tom Pickett. But I can see it ain't him.

ASH. That's right.

PAT. There's only the Kid left . . .

ASH. That's right. (BILLY *has by now stood and taken off his hat. His face is plainly visible.*) You are looking at William Henry Antrim, also known as Henry McCarty, but better known as William H. Bonney, or just Billy the Kid—that's what everybody called him. He is my project.

PAT. (*He stares at* BILLY.) This isn't him.

ASH. Of course it is. I just told you it was.

PAT. He was my friend for nearly four years. I ought to know what he looked like.

ASH. He *looks* like that! He is now 48 and a half years old. You haven't seen him in 26 years, six months and 15 days. Now, how in hell should you know what he's grown up to look like? Hell, you didn't even recognize me.

PAT. Goddamn it, Ash! Don't tell me he's the Kid, 'cause even if he is, he ain't! I killed him! I am the man who killed Billy the Kid. I'm Pat Garrett, damn it, don't you recognize *me?!*

ASH. Look here, Pat. Look at those buck teeth. These teeth were legend throughout the entire Southwest and Northern Mexico! These are the Kid's own buck teeth! If he ain't the Kid, how'd they end up in his mouth? (ASH *is by now holding* BILLY's *mouth open, as one would a horse's.*)

PAT. Lot of people tried this, Ash! Resurrect the Kid, say they seen him in Arizona or Texas, or claim they got his trigger finger in a bottle . . .

ASH. (*To* BILLY.) Stand up straight. He's the Kid's

height—a little shorter, in fact, to allow for the natural shrinking of advancing age. (*Taking* PAT's *gun from the table, tossing it to* BILLY, *who catches it left-handed.*) Left-handed. What was Billy?

PAT. Left-handed.

ASH. Look at those eyes. The Kid's eyes—that shade of blue you can just barely tell is blue. (*To* BILLY.) Take down your pantaloons. (BILLY *gives* ASH *the gun, then takes down his pants. He wears longjohns.*)

PAT. Ash . . .

ASH. Quiet. You're going to see this. Turn around. (BILLY *turns.* ASH *undoes the buttons over the seat. The flap falls.* BILLY *boasts a scar on the left buttock.*) There. There is the selfsame scar that the Kid received in his fabled gun battle on the streets of Lincoln in 1878. Pat, you are staring at the face of history here . . .

PAT. Goddamnit, button him up!

ASH. Button up, Billy. (BILLY *does so, turns around.*) Sorry we had to go so far with it. Tell me, Kid—do you recognize old Pat here? I mean, if you hadn't been told it was him. (BILLY *looks at* PAT, *shrugs.*)

PAT. Can he talk?

ASH. Well, of course he can talk. Can *you?* (*To* BILLY.) Billy?

BILLY. What?

ASH. Explain to Pat how you managed to stay alive all these years.

PAT. He didn't. That's not him.

ASH. Give him a chance, Pat. You've got to admit he bears a resemblance.

PAT. I don't have to admit anything. (*Brusquely, to* BILLY.) Who are you?

BILLY. He's right, all right. I'm Billy the Kid.

ASH. Listen, he knows everything. I've talked to him for hours. I put him through the ringer, and he came out the Kid every time.

PAT. Ash, I won't believe it.

ASH. You'd better. Because he'll make you rich.

BILLY. (*Beginning slowly, then quickening his pace. He shivers throughout, as though he needs a drink. He looks at* ASH *for support at times. Much of the speech has the tone of a recitation badly remembered.*) I, uh . . . well, I was born William H. Bonney in Hell's Kitchen, New York City. I don't remember that too clear, but my mother swore to it. She said Pa left us right about then, and she came west to Kansas, using the name of McCarty—to hide her shame, I guess—and took me and my half-brother Joe along. (*A pause.*) She, uh, she met a man in Wichita named Antrim and married him. They took me and Joe with 'em down to Silver City, New Mexico. (*A pause.*) An' I finished growin' up there, till I was . . . twelve . . . (*Looks at* ASH, *who nods.*) when I killed a man who was coarse to my mother. I killed him with a knife, from behind, and rode out of town so my mother wouldn't be shamed too much by seein' her little son hang right before her eyes. Uh, after that there was many years I just rode around . . . (*Looks again at* ASH, *who gestures him on.*) uh, lyin' about my age an' workin' on ranches mainly. I could ride, shoot an' gamble with the best of 'em. I was mostly over in Arizona then, an' I killed two or three men in poker disputes, an' a lot of Indians, defendin' settlers an' so forth . . . (PAT *gives a disgusted snort.*) Well, then after awhile I killed too many men to stay in Arizona, even though they was almost all Indians. So I rode down into Mexico for awhile, where my fluent Spanish an' expert gamblin' paid off. I killed a monte dealer or two in Chihuahua an' Sonora for my own good reasons, an' . . . uh, rode with a man named Segura.

PAT. Shit!

BILLY. You . . . uh, you may not've heard of him . . .

PAT. Nobody did! Not till Ash invented him and put him in our book. Ash, what are you trying to pull off on me?

ASH. He did exist! Segura was just as real as you or me or the Kid here. Just because . . .

PAT. Shit!

ASH. He knows the whole story, Pat. He's a history book. Knows more than I do.

PAT. (*Staring suddenly at* BILLY.) Joe Grant.

BILLY. What?

PAT. Joe Grant. Who was Joe Grant?

BILLY. Oh. (*He pauses, looks at* ASH *who, unseen by* PAT, *mimes Russian roulette*.) Oh yeah! Uh, I killed Joe Grant in Fort Sumner. (*Laughs*.) That was a mighty funny thing. He was some big-mouth Texas boy who wanted to kill me for the fame, I guess. But he didn't recognize me. Kind of like you, Pat—but he had an excuse, 'cause he never saw me before. Anyway, I knew him though, an' I came up to him in the saloon . . . (BILLY *uses* ASH *for Joe Grant*.) an' I asked him if I could look at that pretty gun he had. (*Indicates the gun in* ASH's *hand*.) It was ivory inlaid. Well, that old woman gave me his gun! (*Takes the gun from* ASH.) An' I looked at it, admired it all up an' down, an' when he wasn't lookin', I set the empty chamber one spot over, so it'd come up next time he pulled the trigger. (*Does so with* PAT's *gun*.) Then I gave it back. (*Gives it back to* ASH.) Then I told him who I was. Well, he turned around an' drew that same gun of his without a single word, an' pointed it right at my nose. (*Takes* ASH's *arm and positions the gun thus, with the barrel resting on his* —BILLY's—*nose*.) Then he pulled the trigger. (ASH *hesitates*.) Pull it. (ASH *hesitates*.) Pull it! I gotta show him! (ASH *pulls the trigger. There is a click*. BILLY *laughs, takes the gun*.) But nothin' happened. So I drew right away before he could shoot again an' nailed him good, here an' here. (*Taps* ASH *on the chest and forehead with the gun*.) He looked real surprised goin' down. (BILLY *sits, sets the gun on the table*.)

PAT. (*Smiling derisively*.) You primed him, Ash. You sat

in a saloon, drank enough to irrigate the territory, and told him everything the Kid ever told you—truth and lies, all in the same bundle. (*Violently.*) I killed him! With my hands, with my eyes, with my brain! (*A silence.*) It sounded like he was reciting your book, minus the poetry.

ASH. Look, Pat. Let the Kid tell you how he escaped that night you think you shot him . . . maybe he'll convince you. You've got to be more open-minded. Don't cut yourself off from wealth untold.

BILLY. You never killed me at all, you know. Well, I guess you can see that. You killed my good friend, Billy Barlow.

PAT. Never heard of him.

BILLY. I know. See, I met him in Arizona, an' we was the town sensation over there, 'cause we looked just alike, right down to the buck teeth. He stayed there in Arizona until that very night when you claim to have got me. See, Billy Barlow knew about me by then, an' found out where I was, too. Just like you did. He was out to kill me, same as you. That's right. That's because we looked just like each other, an' seein' as I wasn't right with the law, that meant he wasn't either, as far as the law could see. Billy was worried about a mistaken identity. He wanted me dead so there wouldn't be no mistakes.

ASH. Keep going, Kid.

BILLY. (*Gaining confidence.*) Well, Billy Barlow caught up with me same night you did, at Pete Maxwell's place. He tried to kill me with a knife 'bout an hour before you showed up. He cut my arm real good, too . . . (*Displaying a scar on his forearm.*) but I got away. He was still lookin' for me when he came into Pete's room a little later. That's when you killed him. Too bad for old Billy Barlow. Died of exactly what feared him. He was innocent as they come, too. I been usin' his name ever since.

ASH. What do you think? Pat, this is one hell of a project. The best I've ever found. This man—this man and you are the two halves of the world for me. And now I've put you together. (*Toasting.*) We are going to make money!

PAT. How, another book?

ASH. (*Ignoring* PAT's *sarcasm.*) That's only part of it. We're going to arrange a tour for you two, as The Greatest Outlaw The West Has Ever Known, Suddenly Found To Be Alive, and The Greatest Sheriff Of Them All. Think of it! A dramatic reenactment of the monumental moment when you two, each the paragon of his chosen field, met in the deadly zone between law and lawlessness—Pete Maxwell's darkened bedroom.

PAT. But he just got through saying I killed somebody else.

ASH. That's a minor point. Pat, for 26 years the picture of that showdown has been engraved on people's minds. It's history. It can't be changed now, so we might as well make something out of it. People won't ask questions; they'll want it to be the way they heard it was. We'll just talk a little faster than usual and nobody'll add it up. (PAT *stares at* ASH.) Well, you're right—they will add it up. But it's not like you didn't kill anybody. You did kill Billy Barlow, and we'll explain that. You see, most of the show will be Billy here, anyway, retracing his deadly deeds and so forth. We'll have the Joe Grant episode, highlights of the Lincoln County War . . .

BILLY. (*Whispering to* ASH.) Fightin' Indians.

ASH. Billy fighting Indians—we'll have lots of Indians, in Europe they love Indians.

PAT. Ash . . .

ASH. But we need you for a climax. Every story has to have a climax. That's the way people are. When you shot Billy, even though it wasn't him, you ended his career. Isn't that right, Kid?

BILLY. Well, yeah . . .

ASH. That *is* right. You didn't kill his body, but you killed his name. That's more important. That's why you're famous. (*Acting it out, glass in hand, achieving by the end some measure of grandeur.*) Now look, now. Try to get a picture in your mind of what this show will be. We'll have banners with yours and Billy's names on 'em, in letters as tall as a man. And we'll have banners with your portraits on 'em, as tall as three men. Just think of that: the face of Pat Garrett staring down at 'em from the side of the stage, striking fear in the hearts of potential evil-doers, while on-stage we present a spectacle of target-shooting, fast draw and rope tricks, just to give 'em a taste of the fast-disappearing West. And then when they're thoroughly primed, when they've seen the Kid move through a life of crime the like of which can only be dreamed of by ordinary men—when they've seen him slaughter 21 good men and true, when they think he can't be stopped, but know he must be stopped, we'll bring out you. You and the Kid. On the same stage. And only Fate between you. That's a dream come true for any lover of the Old West. Pat, they'll be happy to see you up there. They'll want to see you. They've got to see you.

PAT. Oh, for Christ's sake.

ASH. (*Showing strain.*) It's everything you've ever wanted, Pat. Everything you . . . ever hoped for. And I'm here to give it to you.

PAT. He'd look ridiculous. We both would.

ASH. How you look ain't up to you . . . it's up to me.

PAT. I was 30 when I killed the Kid. He was 21. We're both old men—it wouldn't look realistic.

ASH. (*As before, moving toward a chair.*) It's not realism people want—it's the real item . . . I think I better sit down. (*Sits heavily.*) I'm old, you know. (ASH *leans back, closes his eyes—he breathes laboredly.*)

PAT. Ash, are you going to be all right?

ASH. Yes, yes. I just need to . . . rest. You think about it. (ASH *falls silent. His head falls forward.*)

BILLY. (*Rising, examining* ASH's *face, one finger lifting* ASH's *jaw.*) He'll be all right. He gets like this. I gotta take

ACT I AUTHENTIC LIFE OF BILLY THE KID 23

care of him, sometimes. Keep him goin'. He'll make me rich. You too, if you got a brain. 'Cause of me.

PAT. Who are you?

BILLY. You know me. (*Pauses, staring at* PAT.) You want to kill me.

PAT. No, I don't.

BILLY. You sure do. I could always tell that about you, Pat—when you wanted to do harm.

PAT. If I wanted to kill you, I would kill you.

BILLY. You already tried, once. (*With an edge.*) I couldn't believe it when I heard how you killed Barlow. Just shot him down like a cow. Him just standin' there. I never thought you'd do that to me. I mean sure, you held me for hangin', but that's the Territory doin' that, not you shootin' me in the dark. You see the difference there?

PAT. No.

BILLY. I liked you. I loved you. As much as any man. An' you'd do that. Just shoot me. (*Pauses.*) I heard in town you're in trouble.

PAT. From who?

BILLY. Couple people.

PAT. So who am I in trouble with?

BILLY. (*Laughs nervously.*) Someone that doesn't like you, I guess. There's a rich man you owe money. One or two poor ones who owe you.

PAT. Heard any names?

BILLY. Well, Wayne Brazel for one. Hell, it doesn't matter, though. Plenty would kill you for free because you're Pat Garrett. (*Laughs nervously.*) Because you killed me. Main thing is, you should come with us East, where you don't know anybody well enough for them to be your enemies yet. Your kind of man inspires enemies.

PAT. Why should I believe you about anything?

BILLY. (*Sotto voce.*) Because I'm the Kid! An' you know it! An' you know what that makes you. (*Pauses.*) Your only chance is comin' with us. Pat?

PAT. What?

BILLY. I forgive you.
PAT. Who the hell do you think you are?
BILLY. Billy the Kid. I forgive you.
PAT. You son of a bitch, I never even saw you . . .
BILLY. I forgive you.
PAT. Well, I forgive you, you shit! I know who you are. You're a 43-year-old drunk. You've been drunk half your life. I've seen you in every town, hotel and saloon. I've drunk with you. I've been you. Tell me if that's a lie.
BILLY. There's something else I am. I'm Billy the Kid. Now you tell me if that's a lie. Admit it. Admit it's me.
PAT. (*Quietly.*) I know it's you.
BILLY. Well, tell other people, then. Tell Ash.
PAT. Tell Ash? Then who do I tell him I am?
BILLY. Believe me, Pat. I ain't mad at you or nothin'—hell. I'm just glad to see you. Just don't kill me.
PAT. Wake up, Ash. Will he wake up?
BILLY. He should.
ASH. I'm all right. (*Blinking.*) I'm awake.
PAT. How long would this tour take?
ASH. Tour?
PAT. Yeah.
ASH. Two tours. The Domestic Tour and the World Tour. I've worked it all out with some gentlemen in New York City. Make it all in a year or two.
PAT. I'll do it. (*A pause.*)
ASH. You will?
PAT. When does it start?
ASH. Right away! We can leave for Chicago this week. When we get there, we'll be taken care of by some people I've written to. Then on to New York, where we'll start performing the drama of the Great Southwest—and pulling it in.
PAT. (*Staring at* BILLY.) Sounds all right . . .
BILLY. Ash, make him say it's me.
ASH. Hm?

ACT I AUTHENTIC LIFE OF BILLY THE KID 25

BILLY. Make him say it's me. He knows it's me.
PAT. (*Angrily.*) I don't have to say anything . . .
BILLY. Make him say it!
PAT. . . . to, for, or about you, goddamit!
ASH. Now, listen, gentlemen! I don't see where it's so important for Pat to make a lot of public proclamations. Pat, you know who you are, and Kid, you know who you are. Right?
BILLY. I guess I sure as hell do.
ASH. Fine. Let's just go as far as we can, and leave it at that. The paying public doesn't care what we think. It cares what it thinks. Now then, anything else you got to know, Pat?
PAT. Well . . . It has to be a good show. I don't want it all made cheap.
ASH. All what?
PAT. Me killing the Kid. I don't want to cheapen it.
ASH. Why not?
PAT. Why not?!
ASH. It *is* cheap. It *was* cheap. Let's be honest now, between us. There was nothing to what you did to kill Billy. You just sat in a room, and shot the first man who walked in the door. It doesn't take any amount of brains to do that. It doesn't even require much courage. Just an average sense of timing, and in your case, luck. You should be thankful you have the chance at this tour. Few lawmen ever get it.
BILLY. That's right.
PAT. Ash, why do we need him? Why can't I do this tour idea myself? I mean, we know for sure I'm real. But he's suspicious. Damn it, there's got to be a way to do it without him!
ASH. Sorry. He's the big attraction. You'd be along to help complete the picture. But you share 50-50. And I get 25 percent. That's how it is.
PAT. (*Going to the window.*) Anybody come up here with you?

ASH. No.

PAT. Tomorrow morning I'm supposed to ride down to Las Cruces. I'm supposed to meet that fellow Jim Miller down there. He'll be in from Texas; wants to buy the ranch.

ASH. So you think you can sell it as soon as tomorrow?

PAT. (*Nodding.*) If this Miller is a reasonable man.

ASH. That's excellent. We'll be able to travel East in style.

PAT. Ash, what's this tour going to be like, now? I haven't acted . . . I don't know . . . what are we going to do exactly?

ASH. Well, like I say, it'll be the simplest sort of thing we can do. We'll have the two of you reenact the final shootout.

PAT. Could we . . . pace through it one time? Just to get the idea.

ASH. All right. Here, you sit down here. (ASH *seats* PAT *in a chair.*) You'll be able to sit all through the scene, because that's just how you did it in history. Take your gun. (PAT *gets his gun from the table.*) Now Kid, you come up here by the door. (BILLY *does so.*) This is easy money, Pat. This is the Lord's plenty. Now, the Kid had a knife. Is there a knife that Billy here can use?

PAT. Not in here. Can't he use that? (PAT *indicates a wooden spoon sitting on the sideboard.*)

ASH. Sure. This is just a demonstration. (ASH *gives* BILLY *the spoon.* BILLY *brandishes it like a knife.*) Now. For all practical purposes this is Pete Maxwell's bedroom in 1881. It's almost midnight. Kid, I want you to go out there and wait until I call you back inside. Then all you have to do is say, *"Quien es?"* two times and Pat'll kill you.

BILLY. (*Going out, closing the door after him.*) Sure.

ASH. (*Sitting near* PAT.) I'll have to play Pete Maxwell myself, since he's dead and gone, the last I heard. You'll have to pretend I'm lying in bed and the room is pitch-dark.

PAT. What am I supposed to do?

ASH. Well, it's so goddamn simple I almost hate to explain it to you. I am about to call Billy in here. He'll come in, say his line two times, and then you shoot him. Twice, like in history.

PAT. I shouldn't really shoot him, should I? You never did make that clear.

ASH. (*Realizing it, laughing.*) No, I didn't, did I? No, of course you don't really kill him. Just wing him. (*An awkward pause, then* ASH *guffaws.*) Let's go now.

PAT. Ash, what if I kill him? (*A silence.*)

ASH. No tour.

PAT. I couldn't do the tour myself? (ASH *shakes his head, "no."*) I'm within my rights. He's under a death sentence.

ASH. That's a long time ago! Why should you kill him?!

PAT. It was my job.

ASH. Are you crazy!? He'll make you rich, if you let him!

PAT. He'll make me a fool! I'll be the man who *didn't* kill Billy the Kid.

ASH. Pat, people will never forget you killed the Kid, even if it ain't the truth. Hell, it doesn't have to be the truth! It's history!

PAT. (*Shouting.*) Kid!

ASH. You're safe, Pat! You're already in the history book.

PAT. Billy!

ASH. Pat, for me. For me! Here, listen. I've written up some press notices you'll receive. You'll like 'em.

PAT. Billy!!

ASH. "They will astonish the Indies. They will disturb the dreams of Europe. They will shake the ancient traditions of Hindustan . . ." (*After a moment,* BILLY *enters, hesitantly. He shivers.* PAT *raises the gun, takes aim at* BILLY, *then cocks the gun.* BILLY *steps back. A moment passes as* ASH *continues.*) "They will receive the plaudits of hordes of Arabs, whose yells will awake the slumbering Sphinx, which has awaited their coming for forty centuries . . ."

BILLY. (*To* PAT.) Well, pull it. Pull it if you're goin' to.

ACT TWO

Lights rise on the same scene. The door opens, and JIM
   MILLER *appears. He is young, dressed in a dark suit.
   He smiles uncertainly.*

MILLER. Pat Garrett?

PAT. (*Dropping his gun to his side.*) That's me.

MILLER. My name's Jim P. Miller. I'm here about the ranch. (MILLER *extends his hand.* PAT *takes it, shakes it vigorously.*)

PAT. Mr. Miller! Well, why'd you come all the way up here? (*Not waiting for an answer.*) Come on and sit down. I'll pour you a drink. (PAT *holsters his gun, gets a fourth glass as* MILLER *sits.*)

MILLER. I'm not intruding, am I, Mr. Garrett?

PAT. No, no, no, we were just acting . . . just acting something out. (ASH *nods congenially.* BILLY *stares.*) Call me Pat. Nothing's wrong, is it?

MILLER. What?

PAT. The deal's not off, is it? I mean, why'd you ride all this way out into the hills? We're meeting in town tomorrow.

MILLER. No, nothing's wrong.

PAT. Good.

MILLER. I just wanted to see you before we got together in town. I like to get to know the men I do business with.

PAT. (*Pauses, nods.*) Well, fine. (*Suddenly remembering the others.*) Oh, this is a pair of old friends of mine, Mr. Miller. This is Ash Upson, a . . . business partner, and he's . . . (PAT *starts to indicate* BILLY, *then decides to finish his sentence another way, indicating* ASH *again.*) also a novelist. (*To* ASH.) This is Mr. Miller, from Texas. He's here to buy my ranch.

ASH. Pleased.

MILLER. Novelist?

PAT. Ash here helped me write a book once.

MILLER. About Billy the Kid?

PAT. (*Surprised.*) That's right.

MILLER. Well, I sure read that one. Read it twice. (*To* ASH.) Sorry I don't recall you being the author, though.

ASH. Pat wrote it; I just corrected the spelling.

PAT. Oh, Ash wrote it, all right. Then he just accidentally signed my name.

ASH. Well, it got written.

MILLER. (*Indicating* BILLY.) And, ah . . . who are you, sir?

BILLY. Billy the Kid.

ASH. Billy! (*A pause, followed by a laugh from* MILLER.)

MILLER. Billy the Kid. That's good. That's a good joke. You caught me unawares. But who are you?

BILLY. Who I say.

MILLER. Pat?

ASH. Uh, Pat . . .

PAT. He is.

MILLER. I didn't know you were a joker, Mr. Garrett.

ASH. (*Suddenly, with a certain joviality.*) Well, I guess the truth's out. The world had to know sometime. Yes, it's true, Mr. Miller. I know it's impossible, but it's true. Standing before you is the man who killed 21 men in 21 years. Of course, his rate is a little slower these days.

BILLY. Not much.

ASH. Billy.

MILLER. (*To* PAT.) I was under the impression you killed the Kid.

ASH. Oh, he did kill, sir. He did. But it was an imposter Pat killed. The real Billy eluded the law's grasp, and has only recently come out of hiding. He stands here before you, now 48. And he no longer tells how many men he's killed—he's afraid it might make you faint.

ACT II   AUTHENTIC LIFE OF BILLY THE KID   31

MILLER. This true? Pat? (PAT *is silent.*)

ASH. Well, it sure as hell is, isn't it, Pat? This is the biggest news in the Southwest since the death of Billy the Kid. This is the resurrection of Billy the Kid!

PAT. (*Studying his drink.*) It . . . ah, it appears to be true, Mr. Miller.

ASH. He's finally decided to place all his trust in the mercy of the Territorial governor to pardon a life of disrespect for the law.

MILLER. You never killed the Kid?

PAT. Guess not.

ASH. Billy is a hard man, and he's paid a hard price. He's ready to play it honest now.

MILLER. (*Studying* PAT.) You sure he's really the Kid?

PAT. (*With finality and irritation.*) Yes, I said he was!

ASH. Now you seem a bit skeptical, sir. And I don't blame you. But you can take Pat's word for it. Whatever you've heard about Pat, you never heard he was a dishonest man.

MILLER. That's right. You've got a good reputation that way, Pat. (*Rising, approaching* BILLY.) 21 men?

BILLY. (*Nervous around* MILLER.) Then sure. More now. Isn't that right, Pat?

PAT. No.

BILLY. What do you mean, no?

PAT. You never . . . you never killed near that.

ASH. Pat . . .

BILLY. Of course I did! I killed 'em all! If anythin', more'n that—I might've lost track.

PAT. I'd say you killed no more than six.

BILLY. Six! I killed way more'n that!

ASH. Now, Pat—surely you remember more than that. Six—that's a pitiful figure.

PAT. (*A little drunkenly.*) I'm not going to lie, Ash. I will do this, but I . . . won't lie. We're not just talking between us now. This is the public. And if he killed more than six men, he's got to damn well prove it.

BILLY. Six! Hell, I had more'n that before I was 17 years old. I killed more in one day.

ASH. Pat, what are you talking about? What do you want to do?

PAT. I want to tell the truth.

ASH. The truth?!

BILLY. (*Of* PAT.) He's drunk.

ASH. I think maybe we're all a little drunk . . .

MILLER. I'm not.

ASH. Well, of course, I don't mean to . . . Pat, you have to remember more than that. If people thought Billy only killed six gentlemen instead of the scores he really did kill, we couldn't draw flies on our prospective tour.

MILLER. Tour?

ASH. (*With a quick nod at* MILLER.) That's right, the tour. Now, Pat, you have to remember . . .

PAT. Damn it, Ash! You know the truth as well as I do. The Kid wasn't that much of a killer. You know how exaggerated things got. Hell, you exaggerated 'em.

BILLY. I was too a killer! I was! I was! How 'bout the time I broke out of the Lincoln County Jail an' killed those two deputies doin' it? You gotta remember that one, Pat. They was your deputies I killed. (PAT *stares at* BILLY, *who smiles*.) Sure. Ol' Pat caught me somehow at Stinkin' Springs, an' they tried me, an' the Governor never came through on his promise to pardon me 'cause I was more sinned against than sinnin', an' they sentenced me to get hung, an' threw me in the Lincoln County crackerbox they call a jail.

ASH. Kid . . .

BILLY. Quiet, I'm tellin' this! Hell, Pat was guardin' me himself till he had to go up to White Oaks on business. Left me with two truly dumbass deputies—Bob Olinger an' Jim Bell. Them two couldn't keep track of each other, let alone me. (*To* PAT.) You know how I broke out? You never counted on my loyalty among the native New Mexicans. I

ACT II AUTHENTIC LIFE OF BILLY THE KID

spoke Spanish like one of 'em, y'know. I lived with 'em, made all their girls happier'n they'd ever be again—they called me *El Chivato!* That means, "The Kid." (*Pauses for effect.*) Well, them natives slipped me news of a plan, an' I worked it just right. I asked Bell to take me out back to the shithouse, so I could take care of my functions. Well, he did, a' course. Actually, ol' Jim Bell was a good enough gent, an' I just killed him 'cause I had to. Anyway, he took me out there all manacled an' all, an' I went inside the shitter an' reached way down in the hole there for the gun my friends'd left at my disposal. It was wrapped in some pretty smelly newspaper, you better believe! Must've been one of your stories in it, Ash! (PAT *laughs.*) Anyhow, I hid the gun in my pants an' come out again. Bell an' I got halfway up the stairs to the jail, an' I pulled it on him. He saw that thing an' ran as fast as he could, the damn fool. So I had to kill him.

MILLER. You mean you just shot him?

BILLY. Anyway, Bob Olinger was over eatin' dinner an' I knew he'd be up to see about that shot, so I went up to the jail an' found ol' Bob's shotgun. (*Takes the shotgun from off the wall, brandishes it.*) He was a mean bastard. Everybody on Earth hated him. Ain't that right, Pat? Hell, I know it's right. (*He points the shotgun at* MILLER.).

MILLER. Is that loaded?

BILLY. How do I know? Well, I figured ol' Bob'd be comin' over pretty fast, so I waited by the window till he come up the street an' into the yard. Then I shouted down to him, "Hello, Bob! This won't hurt a bit!" (*Calmly.*) An' I shot him with both barrels, 'cause I figured he needed it. (*Pauses, mimes the recoil of a shotgun.*) An' that's the kind of man I am. That's how I go about things. (*Replaces the shotgun.*) How many's that make it, then?

PAT. Six.

BILLY. Six! Now, goddamit, Pat, you even got so old you can't count straight. Now, look. Follow with me here.

(*Counts on his fingers.*) There's Olinger an' Bell, that I just told you about. There's Joe Grant, like I said before; there's Bob Beckwith . . .

PAT. At the McSween house?

BILLY. That's right.

PAT. That was a pitched battle. Must've been 50 men shooting there.

BILLY. (*Ferociously.*) But I got him! An' look there's that Sheriff Brady in Lincoln that me an' the other boys ambushed . . .

MILLER. Ambushed?

BILLY. That's right. You object?

MILLER. No . . .

BILLY. Good. An' I got his deputy Hindman there, too.

PAT. I heard Brewer got Hindman.

BILLY. I got Hindman! I got him! He's part of my 21! An' then there's . . . there's . . . uh . . .

ASH. There's Baker and Morton.

BILLY. That's right! That's right. I killed Baker an' Morton. I sure as Hades . . . killed them . . .

ASH. You remember, Kid. You were taking 'em to jail that time you were a deputy, and they tried to escape.

BILLY. Oh, yeah!

PAT. They weren't escaping. Billy just outright murdered 'em.

BILLY. That wasn't murder! That was vengeance right an' proper! Besides, they're still mine, either way. An' what about Jimmy Carlyle? (*A pause.*) What about Jimmy Carlyle? What about him?

ASH. (*Quietly.*) Billy, he was your friend.

BILLY. My friend? Oh. Oh, that's right. I wouldn't've killed him, then. Them other boys must've killed him.

ASH. That's right.

BILLY. So anyway, that's . . . eight, I guess, right there—not countin' Jimmy. An' I got, uh . . . 13 Indians, so that makes 21. 21. (BILLY *sits, staring straight ahead.*)

ASH. "They will rattle the bones of the Rameses and the Pharaohs . . ."

BILLY. (*To* PAT.) Not the same as it was. I can see you.

ASH. ". . . and rouse feelings of interest in the Eternal City . . ."

BILLY. (*To* PAT.) Make up your mind.

ASH. ". . . not felt since the Coliseum rang with the cries of Christians . . ." (*Suddenly there is a knock on the door and a voice from outside.*)

MILLER. (*From outside.*) Mr. Garrett? Pat, are you there?

ASH. ". . . torn by wild animals."

BLACKOUT

END OF ACT ONE

ACT II AUTHENTIC LIFE OF BILLY THE KID   35

MILLER. That's quite a story . . .

PAT. He's pitiful.

ASH. Now . . .

PAT. He can't remember a thing. Doesn't matter if he's the Kid or not. He can't remember past yesterday!

ASH. He's old. How much do you remember?

PAT. More'n that!

ASH. He's . . . he's had a few problems with alcohol in the last few years, Pat. It's been some trouble to get him to remember what he does. But he does remember. I've watched him. You can see when it comes back to him. His eyes go clear, and then it all flows out of him—you can't stop it, Pat. It's just clear and honest God's truth. Things no one could know. Secrets. The Secrets of the Kid. Pat, he just can't hold 'em anymore. He's real.

PAT. Ash . . .

ASH. (*Sharply.*) He's real! I know what I am, Pat. A voice, and that's all. But I'm Billy's voice. I'm your voice. You and Billy lived great lives, but without me, who would know?

PAT. Look . . .

ASH. Who would know?! Nobody.

PAT. Not so hard to do something great. Just sit in a corner and shoot what moves. (PAT *and* BILLY *stare at each other.*)

ASH. Pat, I better know right now if you intend to treat me honest.

PAT. I'm an honest man. You said so. Right, Mr. Miller?

ASH. You know what I'm talking about.

PAT. I won't kill him, if that's what you mean.

BILLY. You better not. Goddammit, you better not, you stinkin' son of a . . .

PAT. I won't!

BILLY. (*Quietly.*) Not for now.

PAT. (*Having composed himself.*) Hope we're not bothering you with all this, Mr. Miller.

MILLER. I'm amazed.

ASH. What?

MILLER. I'm just amazed, that's all. I come all the way out here to buy a little ranch from a famous man, and look what I walk into. Probably the two biggest names in the American West. Who'd've dreamed I'd live to see Billy the Kid? It's amazing.

BILLY. I *am* him.

MILLER. (*Disarmingly.*) I know. That's why it's so unbelievable. Why, Pat, how long have you known about this?

PAT. Not long.

MILLER. You know, I'd better make an admission about myself. It's true I wanted to get to know the man I'm doing business with, but that's not why I rode 20 miles up here tonight. I would've ridden 200 to shake hands with a man like you, Pat. And you too, Mr. Bonney. I have a respect for men of the Old West that's almost religious. I seek after them. The famous men. The ones who were something. I like to get close to them for a little bit—see what they're like. I like you. Both of you.

PAT. (*Not knowing what to say.*) Thanks.

BILLY. (*Of* MILLER.) What's wrong with him?

ASH. Billy.

MILLER. Just sitting here talking with you I found I like you enough to take a chance with my life.

PAT. What do you mean?

MILLER. I'm going to warn you.

PAT. About what?

ASH. Mr. Miller, what are you talking about?

MILLER. Pat, when I was down in town this evening, I was approached by a number of men. They want to kill you. They warned me to just turn around for Texas again, and never see you. But I couldn't do that.

PAT. Who wants to kill me?

MILLER. A group of businessmen I spoke with.

ASH. Well, why would they want to kill Pat? (*To* PAT.) You know who these men are?

PAT. Yes. One of 'em's a cattleman. I know about a murder he had done. There's a man I beat up when I got drunk in a poker game. Two or three who'd kill anything if it was named Pat Garrett. Who'd you talk to?

MILLER. Well, for one, the man who's going to do the shooting. Wayne Brazel. (PAT *laughs despite himself.*)

BILLY. What's he doin', Ash? What's wrong with everybody?

PAT. Wayne Brazel! Shit, he's wanted to kill me for a year. Says so every time I see him. He's always hated me, my God. He's a bravo, though. A talker. Everybody knows he's the biggest damn coward in the country.

MILLER. Maybe so.

PAT. He is. Didn't anybody down there tell you that?

MILLER. No.

PAT. (*Pausing.*) Well, he is.

ASH. When'd he say he was going to do this, Mr. Miller?

MILLER. Tomorrow morning. On the road into town. You're riding in with him, aren't you?

PAT. That's right. Wayne's coming along. Carl Adamson, too. (*Laughs.*) Is Carl in on it, too?

MILLER. I don't know. Maybe you should take your gun, though.

PAT. I always take a gun. But for Wayne I wouldn't even have to take my hand.

BILLY. What do you do back home in Texas, Mr. Miller?

MILLER. Hm?

BILLY. Back home.

MILLER. Back home? Well, I own some land. Couple ranches. They've been doing pretty well, so . . .

BILLY. Nothin' else? I just like knowin'.

MILLER. Well . . . (*Laughs.*) Well, I'm a deacon in the Methodist church, too. But that doesn't take up too much time.

ASH. Billy, we were discussing something.

BILLY. So am I. I like to know a man. Especially one I

drink with. Especially one who comes in talkin' 'bout ambushes an' murders. You a deacon?

MILLER. That's right.

BILLY. Pretty mild-mannered?

MILLER. (*Graciously.*) Well, I'm a businessman.

BILLY. All the businessmen I ever knew were cowards.

ASH. Billy.

MILLER. It's all right.

BILLY. Don't matter, though. If a man's a coward or brave. Right, Pat?

PAT. (*Losing patience.*) Billy, what are you . . .

BILLY. We're famous. You gotta be careful. Careful who you meet. Hell, Pat, cowards are dangerous! I know. I spent the last eight years tendin' bar, worryin' 'bout cowards, brave men an' those in between. One slip—I was goin' by Billy Barlow, 'course—just once if I'd let 'em know who I really was—any've 'em would've killed me. Brave men, cowards. (*Suddenly laughs drunkenly.*) I told one man, though. Clay Allison. He was mean. He killed 15 men in two years alone. Danced buck naked on top my bar one night. Holes in the ceilin', holes in everybody—an' I told him. Just blurted it right out, drunk. Dumbest thing I ever did. Stood next to that fucker an' said, "I am Billy the Kid. I am." Just like that. Then I started thinkin' about death.

ASH. Kid . . .

BILLY. But he didn't hear me! He was drunk, too! Clay Allison! Ain't that somethin'? Pat?

PAT. Shut up.

BILLY. What I mean to say is, you take a gun, Pat. Them cowards . . .

PAT. I am goin' to take a gun! Now shut up!

ASH. Kid. He's just drunk, Pat.

BILLY. (*With sudden exuberance.*) I am drunk! An' I see. Pat, I see the whole goddam past just like it was, an' we were friends. (*Grins.*) We had a time, didn't we?

PAT. A time?

ACT II AUTHENTIC LIFE OF BILLY THE KID   39

BILLY. *I mean*. Those days were the best part. Some of the women in Fort Sumner, an' drinkin', an' . . . everythin'. Hey, you remember the times we used to rustle cattle an' sell 'em down in Tascosa together?

PAT. That ain't true.

BILLY. 'Course it is, Pat. Hell, we must've done it a hundred times.

PAT. I never rustled.

ASH. Pat . . .

BILLY. (*Cajoling.*) Yes, you did.

ASH. Kid . . .

BILLY. Well, he did. I was right there with him.

PAT. (*Very conscious of* MILLER.) I have been a sheriff, a buffalo hunter, a bartender, rancher, businessman, foreman and a political figure. But I have never broken the law to my recollection, or rustled any cattle. (*Pauses.*) I'll swear it.

BILLY. (*After a pause, quietly.*) He did.

PAT. (*Going for him.*) I never did!

MILLER. (*Stopping* PAT.) I know you're an honest man, Pat.

PAT. I never rustled.

MILLER. That's right.

PAT. I never rustled.

ASH. Let's all just sit down and have another drink.

PAT. (*Sitting.*) I never rustled.

ASH. We know that, Pat.

PAT. Maybe I rustled once. Hell, *he* rustled all the time. He was the goddamn outlaw.

ASH. We know.

BILLY. (*Who has been staring at* PAT.) Shit.

ASH. (*Pouring drinks.*) Mr. Miller, you say you're from Texas? Pretty there. You in West Texas?

BILLY. Shit!

ASH. What?

BILLY. (*Of* PAT.) Look at him, lookin' at me! Look at him! (*With nervous bravado.*) Pat Garrett, you always had a lizard's eyeballs. I ever tell you that? Ash, he's gonna kill me. I know it. I can see his lizard eyes thinkin' over how to do it easiest. An' safest! Givin' me the least chance. Christ, Pat. You just shoot a man in the dark. A man doesn't even know you're there. (PAT *starts across the room for his gun, which is in its holster on the wall.* BILLY *draws a pistol of his own, formerly concealed beneath his serape.* PAT *freezes on* BILLY's *warning.*) I'll kill you!

ASH. (*Striding into the line of fire.*) No one's going to kill anyone!

BILLY. Someone's goin' to kill *some*one. That's how it always is. Somebody's goin' to die. Right, Miller? The minute a man turns his back.

MILLER. I don't see why . . .

BILLY. (*Staring at* MILLER.) Maybe he'll wait. Maybe it won't be tonight at all. Maybe tomorrow, bright an' early. Or after a few days or a few weeks . . .

ASH. Billy, Pat never ambushed . . .

BILLY. (*Fiercely, to* ASH.) You don't even know what a killer looks like! God damn it, everybody's dangerous! Pat, you're just the same. It's goin' to go right by you, an' you're never goin' to see it. Like when you killed me. Right, Miller? You read the book.

ASH. Kid, if you kill Pat, I'll testify against you myself. If you kill him and me and Mr. Miller, you've got one fine road back to tending bar. You like tending bar?

BILLY. I don't know. At least the drinks were free.

ASH. Well?

BILLY. (*Frightened.*) Ash, he'll kill me!

ASH. No, he won't. That wouldn't make any more sense than if you killed him. Neither of you goes on tour without the other one, and neither goes without me. Give that here. (BILLY *gives* ASH *the gun.*) Sit down, Pat. (PAT *gets his gun, sits, polishes it.*) Ranching. That's something I never did try. Like Pat here, I've attempted a number of things in my life. Novels, newspapers—have I told you what I do now, Mr. Miller? I mean right now?

ACT II AUTHENTIC LIFE OF BILLY THE KID

MILLER. No.

ASH. I am an impresario. (*Broad smile*.) And my first production, my first spectacle of worldwide note, will be made up of nothing more than these two men: Billy the Kid and Pat Garrett. Think of it! Thousands—no, millions!—of people paying good money simply to look at these two enemies of old, who as you have seen, can barely keep their hands from each other's throats.

MILLER. What do you intend to do?

ASH. I'm the manager.

MILLER. (*To* PAT.) You're going to perform?

PAT. Well, we discussed doing something like that for a few months.

ASH. 24 months.

PAT. That's right.

MILLER. Do you like the idea?

ASH. Would you like a preview, sir, *gratis,* and I assure you of the rarest and most edifying nature?

PAT. Now?

ASH. Come on, Pat. We've got to start sometime. Best thing in the world, to play for a live audience. Beats a dead one all hollow. (PAT *aims his gun at* BILLY; ASH *takes it away from him, puts it in the holster*.) No, no—remember, you sit down. No need to use your gun. Finger'll do. (*Seats* PAT *in a chair*.) Good. Now Kid, get your weapon.

BILLY. Where's that spoon? (BILLY *finds the spoon, walks outside*.)

ASH. We're creating here before your own astounded eyes the precise moment that Billy the Kid met his fatal doom on July the 14th, 1881, at the hands of Pat Garrett, whom you see here. Now, Mr. Miller, I don't know how much you know about the West . . .

MILLER. I live there.

ASH. No, I mean the *West*. The real West! The land of boundless fortune and infinite danger . . .

PAT. Ash.

ASH. Well, that's what you'll see here. Now, try to imagine it. This is what we call show business. This is the West. (*Slapping his hands together.*) Now, it was night, and Pat had tracked the Kid, armed and deadly, to a ranch in Fort Sumner. Pat was hiding . . .

PAT. I was not hiding!

ASH. Pat was ensconced in a chair in Pete Maxwell's darkened bedroom, muttering with him about the Kid. I'll play the part of Pete, who was asleep at the time. (ASH *pantomimes sleeping.*) Ready, Pat? Kid! Come on in! (BILLY *enters, spoon in hand.* PAT *points his finger like a gun at him.*)

BILLY. (*With poor stage presence.*) *Quien es?* (*A pause.*)

ASH. Go ahead.

BILLY. *Quien es?*

ASH. Come on, Pat . . .

PAT. What'll I do, say bang?

ASH. That's right, for now—till we get some blanks.

PAT. (*Loudly.*) Bang!

BILLY. (*Groaning weakly.*) Oh. (BILLY *slumps to the floor, dropping his spoon. A brief pause.* ASH *stands, approaches* MILLER.)

ASH. Well, there it is. Something you'll probably never see again as long as you live. You can get up now, Billy. (BILLY *rises.*) Well, sir? Give me your honest appraisal of what you've seen here.

MILLER. Well, of course it's been a long time since I've seen a . . . show.

ASH. That's all right. We'll be playin' to folks who haven't even seen an American. Well, I'll let you be. Have a drink; a performance like that must be tiring just to watch.

BILLY. (*To* MILLER.) How was I?

PAT. (*Moving toward his gun in its holster.*) Terrible.

BILLY. Shut up. I'm askin' him. How was I, Mr. Miller?

MILLER. I don't know . . .

BILLY. Was I—you know—real?

ASH. Pat, have a drink here.

ACT II AUTHENTIC LIFE OF BILLY THE KID   43

(*The scene breaks into two conversations: one between* BILLY *and* MILLER, *the other between* PAT *and* ASH.)

PAT. (*Attempting to pass by* ASH *for the gun.*) In a minute.

BILLY. Do I seem real to you; I guess that's all I want to know.

ASH. (*Stopping* PAT.) Now's a good time.

BILLY. I mean, it's been a whole hell of a long time since I was able to act like the Kid. I'm a wanted man. I got to act like somebody else, if I got any brains. That right, Ash? Hell, I know it's right. I was eight goddamn years in Cimarron alone tendin' bar.

PAT. I felt stupid doing that just now, Ash.

ASH. You'll get used to it.

BILLY. Billy Barlow. That's the name I used. That ain't no name at all.

ASH. (*To* PAT.) Hell, I expect both you and Billy will become prime actors.

BILLY. I get afraid sometimes that I really am Billy Barlow. That I just somehow became him when I wasn't lookin'. How was I? Did you get convinced?

MILLER. Of what?

BILLY. That I'm the Kid! I mean, do you stand ready to admit that?

MILLER. Sure, I admit it.

BILLY. You don't believe it. People gotta believe it.

MILLER. (*With surprising anger.*) I said I did.

BILLY. (*Backing off.*) Well, I am. Pat knows. He just won't say. Kill me instead.

MILLER. (*With an obvious attempt to calm himself.*) You know, it seems to me that both you and Pat would fare best if you stopped . . . distrusting each other.

ASH. That's right. You know, I've been . . .

MILLER. I know in the church, trust is the most important thing. Same in business. You have to forget what a man did to you yesterday, so you can make some money with him today. Seems to me at this point in your lives, you should start to open up your arms and . . . accept things. A man's worth a lot more alive than dead.

BILLY. (*Of* PAT.) Huh! He's worth nothin' either way.

PAT. Worth more'n you.

MILLER. I don't see why you should be afraid of Pat, Mr. Bonney.

BILLY. You want to know why? 'Cause Pat knows what that tour'd do to him. Sure. How could he stand it up on that stage for a year with crowds shoutin' nothin' but Billy! Billy the Kid! An' Pat Garrett never got him at all!

PAT. That ain't why I'd kill you.

MILLER. Then why would you?

PAT. Because I'm supposed to.

BILLY. He's crazy!

ASH. Billy, sit down.

PAT. (*Drunkenly, with a smile.*) But I won't do it. Just as long as you know you deserve it, there's no need.

BILLY. You bastard! I'm goin' to kill *you!*

MILLER. You don't need to do that, Mr. Bonney.

BILLY. Why not? Why not? I am someone. I don't know who in hell all you are.

MILLER. You've got no reason to harm Pat.

BILLY. Expect me to sleep again, him knowin' I'm alive? There's no room I'd be safe in. Old Pat's not too bright, you know, but he has one idea. That's kill me. He'll never let go of that.

ASH. You're drunk.

BILLY. Well, drunk I know more'n you. (*To* MILLER.) An' you know more'n everybody. You know more.

MILLER. I don't know any more than . . .

BILLY. I can tell men. Ash, give me back my gun.

ASH. No.

BILLY. You relic! You just sit here an' try to carve up my future like you carve up my past, but you don't know me.

You never in the world believed I was really the Kid. Just some drunk, dreamin' about himself the way he'd like to be. Right? (*Pauses, looks at* PAT.) But Pat knows me. He knows who I am. (*To* ASH.) You got the real one, you fool! How's that for luck!? I am who I am, an' I know it. I don't have to tell myself stories. I rustled cattle; I killed more Indians than most people ever seen; I fought the Lincoln County War, an' would've been a general if they'd handed out ranks. (*To* PAT.) I broke out of every jail in New Mexico, an' I even got away from you. I know what I did, an' I don't owe my name to anybody. They all owe their names to me. I'm gettin' out of here. (BILLY *walks quickly out the door*.)

ASH. (*Rising, hurrying after*.) He walked out the door! (*Calling outside*.) Kid! Come on back! (*Shutting the door*.) Can't see a thing out there. (*To* MILLER.) I'm not worried about Billy. He'll get drunk and hide for awhile, but I'll find him. He'll do things my way. But not Pat. I can see that, just watching them in a room together. (*Showing tiredness, as in Act One*.) I'll just have to get a new Pat Garrett.

PAT. What?

ASH. I'll get an actor, and just tell everybody he's you. It'll work just as well. (*Slumping in a chair, closing his eyes*.) I better rest.

PAT. (*With an involuntary laugh*.) My God.

MILLER. (*After a pause, energetically*.) Well, this is quite a time tonight, isn't it? Haven't had much chance to talk business.

PAT. I'm sorry for all this, Mr. Miller . . .

MILLER. Hell, I've enjoyed it. This is a memorable night for me. All these western heroes—I'll never see anything like it again. But Pat, I'm still worried about you; I mean about your safety.

PAT. (*Motioning towards the door*.) You mean him? He's no . . .

MILLER. No, I mean that Brazel fella. I think he's serious.

PAT. Don't worry about that . . .

MILLER. But I do. I mean, you've—we've all been drinking tonight, and it may not seem real. But think about it. What kind of defense would you have, just riding in like that? I mean, I think about these things all the time. How ambushes work, you know. A man would have no chance at all.

PAT. Against Brazel? What are you talkin' about?

MILLER. No, *not* Brazel. Somebody else. Look, what if it was like this. Brazel says he's going to kill you, rides along with you towards town. Well, you're not too worried, but you keep an eye on him anyway. You keep an eye on *Brazel*—not on anyone else. Not on the man waiting along the way. Brazel knows he's there. Maybe even Carl Adamson knows it. But you don't.

PAT. (*After a pause.*) Oh, that doesn't make any sense . . .

MILLER. It does! I know how it works. Here, let me show you. (*Pulls* PAT *out of his chair.*) Let's just act it out a little—like you and Billy did before. Maybe it'll bring this home, give you a vivid idea. Ash, you help me.

(*He rouses* ASH. *During the following sequence,* MILLER's *demeanor changes radically. He becomes progressively more forceful, more dangerous, more unpredictable.*)

ASH. (*Opening his eyes.*) What? How do you mean?

PAT. Mr. Miller . . .

MILLER. Call me Jim. Now, let's see—let's use the table for a wagon. You're riding in a wagon, that's what Brazel said.

PAT. (*As* MILLER *clears the table, moves it to the center.*) Well, yes, but I don't see why we have to . . .

MILLER. This is—what do you call it—"show" business. I'm trying to show you something. You may be in danger tomorrow, and I want to help you. Now look, Ash, you be Brazel. You'll need a gun. Where's the one you took from the Kid? (ASH *produces* BILLY's *gun.*) Fine. Pat, you won't need this, will you? (*Takes* PAT's *gun, puts it in the holster.*) I mean, you'd probably take this instead, wouldn't you say? Frighten people more. (*Gets the shotgun off the wall.*)

PAT. I . . . might.

MILLER. Sure you would. Is it loaded?

PAT. No.

MILLER. (*Tossing it to* PAT.) Doesn't need to be. (*Patting the table.*) Sit in the wagon.

PAT. (*After a pause.*) All right, let's see this. (PAT *sits on the table.*)

MILLER. Now, we need some killers. Carl Adamson'll be driving, probably too close to do the job, sitting next to you. We'll just pretend he's there.

ASH. Where?

MILLER. (*Slapping the table hard.*) Right here! Try to imagine it! Brazel's riding a horse?

PAT. That's right.

MILLER. Fine. Ash, you'd be right over here, then. (*Positions* ASH *a few paces from* PAT.) Now, you're on a horse, remember. (*Stands* ASH *on a low stool.*) And you have a gun. Pat, look at him. Smile, Brazel. You know Pat doesn't have a chance. (ASH *attempts a smile.* MILLER *moves to the side of* PAT *opposite him.*) I know everything about an ambush. Must've read a million books. Pat? (PAT *looks at* MILLER.) He's Brazel, that's Carl Adamson next to you, and you're you. Right?

PAT. Right.

MILLER. Brazel, raise your gun up there—aim it at Pat.

ASH. Well . . .

MILLER. Do it! You hate this man! (ASH *does so, slowly.*) That's right. Pat, you know who I am. The ambush! Hard to say who it is—some friend of Brazel's, maybe. Or a professional. Who do you think?

PAT. Does it matter?

MILLER. No. You're right. Could be anybody. Nobody with a name you'd remember. Brazel, got your gun up?

ASH. Yes.

MILLER. Me too. Now, Pat—put yours down.

PAT. But, he's got a gun on me.

MILLER. But you don't think he'll use it. Besides, Carl's stopped the wagon. Says he wants to check the traces—says they're tangled. So, you're just sitting, and maybe you decide to get out and stretch and piss or something. You do that now.

PAT. Stretch or piss?

MILLER. It doesn't matter. (PAT *stands, stretches.*) Yeah. Now, keep an eye on Brazel. And while you're doing that, I'm up here in the brush, and you can't see me.

PAT. All right . . .

MILLER. But I hate you. More than Brazel does. Maybe I don't even know why I hate you. Maybe just Pat Garrett's name in all those books they write, made bigger than it is, seeing it over and over . . .

ASH. Mr. Miller . . .

MILLER. Hold that gun up, Brazel! Pat, you got one chance, and that's get to a gun quick. How you going to do it?

PAT. How am I . . . ?

MILLER. How!? You got to live. Find a way!

PAT. I don't have to do anything!

MILLER. (*Producing a pistol from under his coat.*) Then you're going to get killed.

PAT. Why?!

MILLER. (*Swiftly, levelly.*) Pat, I am a very religious man. I believe everybody should have a chance. But if I was the man who ambushed you tomorrow, I'd be all business.

PAT. *Why?!*

MILLER. Because I hate you! They hired me to come all the way from Texas and shoot you in the back of the head, but Goddamit, I would've done it for free! (PAT *stares at* MILLER *for a second, then fakes a dive for the shotgun, and moves instead for his pistol on the wall.* MILLER *fires a shot into the floor ahead of* PAT, *who spins away and crouches.* MILLER *slowly takes aim at* PAT, *waits a long moment, then puts his*

ACT II AUTHENTIC LIFE OF BILLY THE KID 49

gun back in his coat. His tone is subdued.) Not time enough. You'd be dead.

PAT. Christ.

MILLER. (*Putting his gun away.*) That's how it could happen. That's all I'm saying. (BILLY *rushes in suddenly.* ASH *automatically aims at him.*)

BILLY. Who shot?

MILLER. Just a game.

BILLY. Ash, give me my gun. He is a killer. Pat, he is! (PAT *moves quickly for his pistol, aims at* BILLY.) Ash!

PAT. (*To* BILLY.) Who am I?

BILLY. Ash!!

PAT. Who am I!? *Pat Garrett!* (PAT *fires, hitting* BILLY *in the chest.* BILLY *falls with a scream, and dies.* PAT *stares at him, as does* MILLER. ASH *approaches* BILLY.) Is he dead?

ASH. Yes. (*Silence.*)

MILLER. Well, I should probably be getting back. (MILLER *gets ready, starts to leave.*)

PAT. Mr. Miller. (MILLER *stops.*) I'll, uh . . . see you in town tomorrow.

MILLER. You'll see me. Good night, Mr. Upson.

PAT. (*As* MILLER *opens the door, pointing at* BILLY.) No need to . . . remember him.

MILLER. I don't have any business with him. (MILLER *exits.*)

PAT. No tour.

ASH. You'll die a failure.

PAT. I'll die after him. (PAT *pours a drink.*)

ASH. There's no money in you. Why didn't I know a thing simple as that?

PAT. (*As* PAT *continues,* ASH *puts on his coat and hat, goes out the door without looking back.*) We did a little drinking tonight. I used to get drunk like this all the time, in El Paso. Me and some friends. Had a lot of friends down there—especially ol' Tom Powers. Tom was a good friend.

Owned a saloon. Called it, "The Coney Island Popular Resort." We'd all get drunk. (*Hearing the door close behind* ASH.) You can stay here tonight; it's cold out. (*Goes to the door, looks out, closes it again, looks at the corpse.*) Well, you'll stay, won't you? You would've liked ol' Tom Powers. Think I'll go down there again, when I sell this place. (*Picks up the shotgun, puts it away.*) He'll be happy to see me. Free drinks. Know what I'll tell him? (*Raising the pistol.*) "I am the man who killed Billy the Kid. Twice." (*Drops his arm, sits heavily, knocks over an empty glass.*) This place startin' to look like the Coney Island Popular Resort. (*Suddenly wheels and aims his gun at the corpse.*) You moved! (*The corpse hasn't moved.*) Don't move. Don't. (*Fade to black.*)

CURTAIN

END OF ACT TWO

THE END

MUSIC USE NOTE

Licensees are solely responsible for obtaining formal written permission from copyright owners to use copyrighted music in the performance of this play and are strongly cautioned to do so. If no such permission is obtained by the licensee, then the licensee must use only original music that the licensee owns and controls. Licensees are solely responsible and liable for all music clearances and shall indemnify the copyright owners of the play(s) and their licensing agent, Samuel French, against any costs, expenses, losses and liabilities arising from the use of music by licensees. Please contact the appropriate music licensing authority in your territory for the rights to any incidental music.

IMPORTANT BILLING AND CREDIT REQUIREMENTS

If you have obtained performance rights to this title, please refer to your licensing agreement for important billing and credit requirements.

www.ingramcontent.com/pod-product-compliance
Lightning Source LLC
Chambersburg PA
CBHW071845290426
44109CB00017B/1931